Red Mud

_____

Patricia Goodrich

VIRTUAL ARTISTS COLLECTIVE
http://vacpoetry.org
ISBN: 978-0-9798825-9-3

Acknowledgment is made for poems published earlier in *An Intricate Lacing* (Nightshade Press), *Papered Rooms* (Still Waters Press), *Sidelights* (Kali Moma Press), *Fur Flesh Bone* and *Mosser Street* (Petoskey Stone Press), and Druskininkai Poetic Fall 2005.

Some of these poems were written during residencies at Atlantic Center for the Arts, Europos Parkas, Santa Fe Art Institute, Vermont Studio Center, and Yaddo. To those organizations and to the Pennsylvania Council on the Arts, the Puffin Foundation, and the Andy Warhol Foundation who supported my work, I am grateful.

As readers and friends, poets Christopher Bursk, Elizabeth Raby, and Steven Schroeder have helped shape this manuscript and in many ways my life.

for my daughter Laurel H. Walton
& my son Trapp R. Heydenberk

Table of Contents

Clay

Doe in Autumn...8
Cells...9
Drawstring...10
Defining the Dark...12
Vinegar Water...15
What the Woman Had Forgotten..............................16
Blue Melton Coat..17
Mid Night Wakenings...18
Clay...19
Sidelights..21
Amputee..22
On Viewing "The Punishment of Tityus".....................23
On Burning a Bird...24
Bones...25
Matter of Substance...26
Stripping Sheets...27
Rings..28
On Burning a Dog..29
Boundaries..30
Passover Moon..32
The Cripple...33
The Day Before Muzzleloader Season..........................34
Random Shafts..35
Atonal..37
Guardian Angel...38
THE TRUTH...40
Miniscule Matters..41

Muck Land

Spoor..44
Bear...45
Father..47
A Game of Stretch...48
Blue Parakeet..50
The Left Hind Foot...51
Soft-Mouthed..52
Celery...53
What My Mother Told Me...............................54
The Woodchuck's Lot.......................................55
Pulling the Brass Handle..................................56
Springing the Trap..57
First Night..58
Releasing the Safety..59
Clean Shot...61
Gutting the Deer...62

Red Mud

ink..64
Quail...65
Deer..66
Moose Encounter...67
Midsummer Night..68
I wrote a poem about meeting Allen Ginsberg,..............69
Numbers...72
The River Place..74
Flesh Tones...75
Dear Laughter..76
Fox..78
Holey Tree..79
Owl...81
Five Feathers..82
Turning Stones...83
Wild Turkeys..84

Homecoming in February... 85
White... 86
Rut...88
To a Friend... 89
Temptation... 91
Hybrids... 92
What's in a Name...94
Directions for Maps Without Boundaries...................96
Locus..98
The Way Home.. 99
In Praise of the Dolphin... 101
Woodchuck... 103
Fragments of Bone... 104
Ice Defined... 106
Another River Place... 108
The Design.. 109

Clay

Doe in Autumn

Why not the roadside's red
sumac with full umber stalks?
Why the raw pink tongue
unfurled above the twisted
neck, a passing sight
seconds in view,
with me from
crimson morning
sun until tonight's
bleeding moon,
as if I could make
a difference, as if
I were she, as
if her tongue
were mine
or someone
who has licked me,
as if somehow
there is a connection,
somehow it matters?

Cells

I think about it sometimes:
My leg being burned,
tossed into some hospital incinerator,
gone to ash ahead of me;
how at that moment
I never knew the difference.

I mean, it would seem
that even disconnected
I would have felt its pain,
that those cells wrested away
would call to sister corpuscles
in their burning moments, and
I would miss myself,
at least a little.

But I'm all here,
wondering how I can feel
complete
and yet a part of this body
to which I've grown accustomed,
wondering how much you can cut off
and still be whole.

Drawstring

A suspect sweet smell,
thick as the pink syrup
my mother-in-law insisted
no medicine cabinet should be
without. Good for you
whether you liked it or not.

Go. Take a look. See
what you did to her. Words
I didn't hear his mother say
after she helped maneuver me—awkward,
unsure of where to place hands
to bear weight—into the bathtub

for the first time after the accident.
He hadn't told her or his father
about the 1200cc Harley stashed
in his cousin's garage. Moved
to our house when we married.
Hidden away each time they visited.

He didn't open the door.
I wouldn't have wanted him to.
No more than I wanted her
witness to the unseemly
unwinding of the Ace bandage
and the thick angry wound
tacked by black stitches.

For years his eyes found somewhere else
to look. His fingers didn't stray
to the stump. I kept my leg covered
long after the flesh puckered
as if pulled by a drawstring
and the cut across my knee
healed itself into a crooked grin.

Defining the Dark

I.

She doesn't remember the accident.
Her husband told her the details
of car and cycle, ambulance and amputation,
even showed her the stretch of road and
cursed the drunk who had hit them.
She is thankful for whatever chemicals
her body produced that allowed her to forget.
But the other, self-inflicted amnesias....

Mornings after, she reads family faces
for clues. Has she offended?
Calls friends, pieces fragments
of missing hours, pretends she recalls
conversations, jokes, whole movies.
The holes like those in her dreams
—stairways with missing steps.

II.

It isn't as if she drinks anything
stronger than beer or wine. She doesn't
like the taste of most liquor.
It should be simple to quit.
(To be sure that she can
she stops smoking cigarettes.)
At least her drinking isn't costing
her family a lot. She drinks cheap wines,

buys by the gallon, measures red
against white, the unit price,
quart versus liter, sweet versus dry.
For company, she selects by the shape
of the bottle, how pretty the label.
Italy, a picture she favors.
She doesn't go to bars.
Her husband no longer
invites her to faculty parties.

She doesn't drink mornings, and only
on Sundays does she start sipping at noon.
Mostly she waits until cooking dinner.
Meals are prepared earlier, that's true.
But no one says anything—
their children, her friends or his.
Certainly not him.
They never argue. Just talk
less and less.

III.

Things creep outside
the corner of her eyes. No matter
how fast she turns, dark shapes
disappear. She labels them:
Rat Mouse Cockroach.
When she curls in bed, voices
vibrate from invisible walls.
Leftover radio waves, she tells herself
and tries to ignore them.

She's glad they don't carry a message
directed to her. Voices talk to her mother
about mutilated bodies and politicians' plots.
Paranoia, schizophrenia, manic depression
—the daughter searches books for which
applies and the odds of inheriting it.
She ignores her father's alcoholism.
There is a big difference between
being crazy and being a drunk.

Vinegar Water

Alone, I clean the house
to make it nice for me,
   not because I should
   or because I'm angry
        like I used to scrub
        the kitchen floor on knees,
        rinse with vinegar water
        the way my mother trained me,
        wax by hand, stroking smooth
          the ripples,
        bend eye level, buttocks raised,
        hair brushing the floor
        to spot any dull spots
        I might have missed.
  An act of aggression,
        the only violence
        I allowed myself
        those days as wife.
This may seem odd
to you,
   you who came home
   to shining floors,
        the acid clean smell
        of work done well,
and mistook its surface
for love.

What the Woman Had Forgotten

The woman lied without knowing when she told
a friend she had never kept a journal,
not recalling the sheaf of papers squirreled
away in the attic of a leased house,
moved there from another attic she bought
then sold after the divorce. The journal she had
camouflaged in a children's fiction folder
in a file cabinet he rifled through while
custody and property division were pending.
True, she hadn't thought of it as a journal
when she made the daily entries. It was
what she had to do to remember anything
of the day before, no less the past
week, or appointments for tomorrow.
Details of living—whom she saw,
what was said; numbers—her own phone,
the date he left, the cost of everything
she bought. What she did
to make order from the chaos. No.
To bear witness to her own life. No. No.
To keep from feeding her daughter
the same thing, days in a row.

Blue Melton Coat

For Laurel

Mother,
whose distant daughter
fights to gather
a coat about her
and turns her back
to button it by herself,
don't fight.
Let her button
the blue Melton coat
trimmed in beaver pelt,
a coat you made,
the child so much like yourself,
wanting to find her
own way, make
her own order.
Give her time
to angle the awkward
buttons through whipped edges.
There is no match
between an uneven
hem and the symmetry of her
walking proudly by your side.

Mid Night Wakenings

The dog barks.
I pull a wool sock over my stump,
slide it into the rubber liner,
then lean into the leg.
I shift my weight forward
and stand to tighten
the velcro strap above my knee.
Two o'clock in the morning.
The collie is more than half blind
and nearly deaf, this dog
I've neglected lately,
feeding her certainly
but leaving her hair
to weave itself into mats,
spraying her occasionally
but not picking off the ticks attached,
heads buried bloating themselves.
Perhaps because she was left behind
with me. Whatever the reason,
I don't like this
new ritual of mid night wakenings,
nor standing by the back door,
clapping hands into the dark
waiting for her to come.
I don't like watching her
weave up and down the driveway
till she homes to the sound,
stumbles up the steps,
bumps into the screen door,
trying to find a way in.

Clay

The Reds didn't disappear
all at once. Two gone, then three,
until by week's end their coop
was empty.

Plucked by raccoon, weasel, skunk
or perhaps the family retriever,
less tame now the man and boy
were gone.

Following a feathered trail,
the woman knew she'd find carcasses,
necks askew, clipped wings angled
as if for flight.

She bagged the bodies,
scooped fans of feathers,
hoped the daughter would accept
another fairy tale: lost in the woods.
What were a few hens, more or less,
scratching here and there?

The man had recognized the beagle
was dying, but no one wants death
hounding him, though it trails
without an invitation.

Left behind, old and its kidneys failing,
hunting companion, for years
closer to the man
than the man was to the woman.

By small game season, the dog lay
stiff on ground barely frozen.
She turned the earth in a field where
he'd chased rabbits in circles
till, tired of the game,
they holed.

A cold spell. The two cats disappeared.
Days of searching, crying *herekittykitty*,
making up tales of where they might be:
catnapped or with some new cat lovers.

Finally found stretched on their sides,
legs extended in the beagle's abandoned house.
Cause of death: rat poison, most likely.
The funeral: ceremonious.

Winter hardened into February.
Kennel cough caught the last two beagles.
Cardboard boxes gave way to hefty garbage bags.
Against the slanting sun, the woman chinked red clay,

but the litany rang shallow.

Sidelights

it is the things
                    that come at you
sidewise
            that get you
the car   crossing   an intersection
  a girl
    heading
      downhill
        pedaling
          her brother's
                brand-new
                    three-speed
                          bike
                    backwards
              not remembering
          how to
      stop
  lights   on a highway   nothing else   lights
sli
cing
side
vision
      a young woman
                  torn
              off   a 1200 cc Harley
          mangled
    remembering

                  nothing
                      but
                                light

someone you love   leaving   without saying
                                        goodbye

——————

21

Amputee

twenty-five years
without

five years reading aloud
a poem

in which I wrote
the wrong name

for the missing
bone

fibia
where

fibula
should be

On Viewing "The Punishment of Tityus"

Michelangelo, you knew
what made the picture was
not the man
nor the beast of a bird
but the grip that bound
them together.
And so the talons
with their spurs—softly
sketched—a study
in pain and pleasure.

        Oh crow, would that
        you had talons to
        clutch the little beasts
        and carry them away.
        Instead this splayed
        foot that beggars itself
        cannot even grasp
        enough to prey.

Yet, when Michelangelo
reversed the paper,
turned and traced
his other side—
manChrist resurrected
reaching one hand open
toward the sky—the other
remained lowered,
clawlike at his side.

———

On Burning a Bird

Its body rigid, singed
feathers glazed grey with ash,
legs stiff, unjointed sticks like
those cartoon crows Heckle and Jeckle
or a farmer's cat lying flat
on a double yellow line.

Foolish bird, flying into the flames
instead of following smoke's
curled trail up the flue
toward blue sky.

Foolish woman, believing the stranger
and lighting the fire
to drive it out.
What kind of a house
were you protecting
from a wayward starling?

Bones

I've carried this thing
for bones too far.
                Last night
I gathered dreamsful,
a brown shopping bag
tearing under their weight.
Nothing else to carry them in.
                And somewhere
my children coming home
with no arms to greet them.
I needed to be there
before they arrived.
                But I couldn't
leave the bones—
the white winged blade
lifting away from
a broken cage,
nor the pelvic cradle
split.

Matter of Substance

Today I face the mirror
full length, see
the withered stump
as you must,
and regret the rest.
You may say you don't
miss it, its absence
makes no difference.
But this is ugly.
There is no other
word for it, a dangling
modifier, shrunken
like an enemy's skull
saved by headhunters
of the Solomon Islands.
                    Unlike
a cypress's knobby knee
or the gnarled roots
of trees on Franconia
Notch, whose twists
wrinkle the paths
and catch an unbendable
ankle unaware,
this leg is not
attached to earth.
No roots suck nutrients.
All it can do is
feed on itself.
This is my body.
Take it.
Take it.

Stripping Sheets

Why turn away from the birthmark
of menstrual stain? Read
like a Rorschach blot,
what might it say to her....to him?
Does she close her eyes, turn
from the evidence of her failure
to conceive? Is he relieved?
Or does he see it as a sign of the week
to come, neither needing to make
excuses or feign sleep?
Does she remember wakening
to the sticky clots between her legs,
hoping the ring hasn't spread?
Or are the memories sweeter?
Flush with the warmth of her sex,
does she blot herself, shift onto
his fresh side, and, gyrating her pelvis,
rub her pubic bone, massage her clitoris
against his buttocks, his thighs?
Does he recall that richer musk of her
when she bleeds, the swelling welcome
of his seed, the red-flecked mucus
that clings to him when he withdraws?

Rings

She always believed she was good at signs.
Both times she knew when she was pregnant
almost from the start.
She watched for rings around the moon,
red skies at night, woolly bear harbingers of heavy snow,
moss on trees' south sides foreshadowing thaw.
She marked the tracks of foxes....a single trail in fall and winter,
crisscrossing pairs near spring.

His signs were there for weeks and months:
Measured courtesies, lovemaking with barest touch.
Yet she did not read them,
ascribed the changes to the phase of their lives.
Too anchored perhaps in the pull of moon,
the natural cycle of the seasons.
Too dependent upon creatures
to be faithful to their habits.

On Burning a Dog

For a day she and her daughters try to bury him, but they live on rocky ground, and the dog–he's big and black, part Lab—won't fit into any hole. They hit rock, find another spot and try again until they break the shovel's point. By now the dog is stiff, and the day is stinking hot; flies are beginning to swarm, and she's worrying about maggots. Out back there's a place where they pile sticks (sticks Pepper probably chased) and whatever else will burn in a bonfire. It's just before the Fourth of July, so she decides to light it early— after all, she says, they burn people in India, so it can't be too unholy, and it would be sanitary.

Surly, her girls don't want any part of this. They leave her alone, except for disparaging remarks they throw out like old bones. She drags poor Pepper to the pile, him feeling heavier than the sixty pounds he started out to be. (She's a bit more than double that and barely five feet three, but strong—her husband had a stroke before he died of cancer a couple of years back, and she took care of things.) She grabs Pepper by two stiff legs, heaves him high, and poles him until he's centered on the pyre. Then she says a prayer and touches off the tinder, smoke and flames turning blue as the wood catches fire.

It singes fur, but his body doesn't want to burn, so she splashes him with gasoline, expecting the kind of torch she'd seen on TV when Vietnam was news and nuns and monks and ordinary people set themselves on fire. But though the body flamed, she says it took all night for him to disintegrate. Even in the house, doors and windows closed, singed hair and ash of bone reeked through nose and mouth, permeated her pores.

Boundaries

It isn't as if the wings are clipped.
Simply she doesn't spread them.
Holds them close, fans folded,
as if their warmth is her
only protection.
The bird is poised outside
my second-story study
in a crook of limbs that look
as if it could not support anything
heavier than leaf.
Certainly not this stony grief
that seems to weight her.
She isn't frozen in the nest.
She could move if she wanted.
There are no more eggs
to tend, nor for that matter,
any mouths to feed, no
gaping orange wounds
calling for her
to fill their need.
But no reason,
either, for her
to leave.
She's become stilted
even in the sounds she makes,
a pattern of unfamiliar
staccato broken
by odd silences.
Under wings and down
lies a shrunken chest,

but behind the gauze of eyes
something binds her,
brooding, close to nest.

Passover Moon

I am the woman of the white moon.
So cold is its light, no steaming mist rises.
Yet my vision distorts in its wash.

Deer of the meadow become ghosts grazing
on moon's flash-frozen fields.
Do their tongues burn
as they curl around icy glassed spears?
How boldly they stare.
I am the stranger, the intruder here.

Maidenhairs etch my forehead deeper than skin,
pressure unfurling leaves' lattice design.
Were there a lover,
would his mouth moisten my brow?
Would his fingertips trace
midrib's pithed ridge?
Oh, that this mirror were not full!

The pond glazes into a clear dance floor,
surface so shiny that I want to be
the first to waltz, even alone,
to swirl in white gauze without stumbling.
To be wholly beautiful
if only for a moment's balance.

The Cripple

Clearly he is mutilated, this deer
who strips ivy from a tree in the side yard,
approaching with the herd closer than I've ever seen.

His left hind leg dangles, twisted,
hoof reversed, almost severed at the joint.
Ignored, but not shunned, he makes his three-legged way.

I've watched yearlings, doe, and jousting buck
through the rut and hunting seasons,
but this is my first glimpse of the cripple.

I notice the whole body now.
No antlers jut from its crown.
The deer is a doe. I have to leave the window.

The barometer's falling, a sleet storm
predicted, probably what pushed her and the herd
close to the house before seeking refuge in the cedar swamp.

Its roots and vines catch my wooden ankle
and trip me when I walk. She could stumble
on those scarred paths. Freeze or die of gangrene.

I don't own guns anymore.
Anyway, I doubt I could finish her off.
If my son were here, maybe I'd ask him to shoot her.

———

The Day Before Muzzleloader Season
for Trapp

He studies the deer on bended knees
behind a bubbled attic window.
Their bodies float like apparitions
from the woods over the mown field.

Except for the impertinence
of white flags raised,
they graze like domestic beasts,
not cousins of gazelle.

For almost an hour my son kneels,
watching them until their numbers
swell to a dozen, then dissolve
in the gathering dusk.

He breaks the silence once,
whispering to whatever
God inhabits attics
or a young man,

I shouldn't be seeing them now.
It will jinx me tomorrow.

Random Shafts

From what angle to take the picture?
One triangular ear
and a ravaged haunch exposed from snow.

One deer. Nothing like the stories
my son tells,
dozens starved and frozen in remote hills.

I circle, careful my footprints won't mar
the shot.
Then tag a cedar with a blue plastic strip

to mark the body, for return come spring
to gather
the bones for my own purposes.

Eyes to ground, with no particular
destination,
I cross from one cleaved path to another.

Crust breaks under my heavy load.

Gray down and pin feathers lie under
low-limbed spruce.
The calligraphy of a recent kill.

Curled wisps cluster in crosses.
Random shafts.
One small pink circle melting snow.

I'll glean the feathers, but not until
I take time
to photograph the pattern of death.

Soft down clings to the dry ridges
of my fingertips.
Too light to let loose; no body to hold onto.

Atonal

At night in bed fingertips touching,
I try to say my prayers perfectly
as if to atone for my own imperfection,
determined to offer undivided attention
if not a fully contrite heart. How hard
it is to keep my hands from falling and
to recite flawlessly the first time through.

My fingers fumbled over the buttons
of a 120 bass accordion my parents bought
so I could learn to play barrel-roll polkas
Grandma loved and march down Main Street with
Mrs. Sogge's all-accordion band in the Fourth of July parade,
a luxury my mother sold when Dad failed to pay
support, one I replaced thirty years later,
driving my daughter to distant lessons
to mute the discord in our home.

Each time my mind strays
I make myself pray
to the *Amen*
before beginning
Our Father again.

Guardian Angel

*Jesus loves me. This I know...*A girl sings hymns
as she passes beneath the boughs of oak and maple.
It is past shadow, past dark, beyond the reach
of street lights. She wants to believe singing
without repeating verse or song
will take her safely down to the corner
and deliver her home again.
*This little light of mine...*Lights burn
in the first houses. Neighbors she knows sleep
on the far side of curtains, close enough to hear
if she has time enough to scream.
Onward, Christian soldiers...
The big oak, the halfway mark, stands solid
in front of her best friend's house.
Its porch swing creaks, mixing with the broom-bristle
sweep of leaves. Sweetly familiar.
*Swing low, sweet chariot...*She tries to quiet
her footfalls and lowers her voice till the sound
can be heard only in her head.
She stretches out the last words till the next
sound is settled on, so no deadly silence
will intervene and He might think
she's broken her pact.
*Whispering hope...*past the alley,
lengthening her stride....
Do Lord, Oh do Lord....
She stops.
Almost in the arc of the corner light,
she hangs back, fearing someone
will see her waiting.

She doesn't dare stop singing
but strains to hear another sound—
her mother's steps, cushioned in white waitress shoes,
coming home from Johnny's around the corner
down the street, coming home....
afraid to walk alone.

THE TRUTH

of the matter
is my faith
may be more
a matter of
habit, rote
like a rosary.
Think of nuns
who fingered
black beads, wearing their own black habits with white cowls, setting
an example impossible to follow, moving at a measured pace as if
they didn't occupy their lives, their minds and hearts set on something
someplace, some-
one higher than
we could ever
reach. Theirs
a duty: we the
cross they bear.
Do not cross the
line. Walking
with eyes to
ground, they do
not trip, nor skip.
A habit easier
to follow.
Step on a crack,
break your mother's
back still ringing in
my ears, along with
Our Father & Hail Mary.
Mother, are you listening?

Miniscule Matters

Suspended
in the middle
of the kitchen floor,
paws dangling like unanswered question
marks against the white stripe of belly,

he was no coward, or perhaps pain
took him beyond issues of bravery.
Two drops of blood tethered him
just feet from the brown box of bait.

Thus our paths crossed, and I gave way.
Although the power of mercy was within reach
with one swift swoop of broom, I left
and ate supper at a diner,
anticipating his body
inert on its side,
blood flooding to
a mouse-size
pool.

At home, the body
was no longer malleable.
I swept it onto a red dustpan,
carried its weightlessness at arm's length,
flung it into the brittle weeds, hoping
the great horned owls that scavenge
the field would find him
before he rotted, forgetting
what poisons one
poisons another.

Muck Land

Spoor

Brown paper bag in hand
she scans the forest floor
for fungus,
rootless white puffs
that open their capes
and release their seed.
Long after green leaves
succumb to frost,
she gathers tiny wizened
cups that hug the ground
in scatterings,
seeks fluted edgings
thriving on fallen birch,
finds fan and fern
and orange-red ripples.
She gathers them
as if she can harvest
the powers of decay,
dry brown leaves
returned to loam,
rich fertile rot.
As she walks the woods,
the fungus does not rustle
like the leaves—
No, its flesh breaks
silently.

Bear

The bears came back last night
though the night itself was starless.
I saw them from a distance—
two cubs closer and a sow
emerging from the brush—
but their presence was enough
to make my body grow rigid
like the hairs that guard
their humpback necks.

When I was young,
they came near every night
till I feared the terror
that waited behind closed eyes.
Brown bears sprung from rivers,
huge paws spearing fish
until they spotted me.
Black bears laid hillside ambush.
Surrounded, I had to travel.
There was no other way.
I'd wake shaken,
exhausted by my flight.

They say you can't hunt bear long
before he's hunting you.
He circles, creeping up behind.
Despite his size, he moves
with stealth, quietly.
Years have lapsed
since they lost my trail—

marriage and children covered track—
but now they have my scent again.
Now the bears are back.

Perhaps their appearance is a message
from some restless Chippewa spirit
bound by broken treaties.
Perhaps the bear lives within,
banished to some secret place
all those years I was secure.
Perhaps I've grown weak.
Perhaps he senses wounds,
and I seem a likely prey.
I've heard that if you strip
the fur of bear away,
the naked frame looks human.

Father

I never liked the bear hugs
that you gave me,
the whisker burns you
chafed against my cheeks
like a grizzly scratching
his humpback, rubbing bark
off shagged hickory.

But I never said, afraid
the words once spoken
would suffocate the flame
that sparked between.

I never said I'd rather
have you tuck me in, say
Our Fathers, kiss my forehead,
bring me glasses of clear water.

I chose stone over water,
settled for scraping flints.
Friction became the current of our days.
Bear dreams filled my nights.

A Game of Stretch

A brother and sister stand three feet apart and face each other.
She lobs a jackknife underhanded as far as she can,
watches as an arc of its blade cuts ragged patches of light.
She hopes without faith that the game will end quickly,
that he can't keep one foot on the ground and slide the other
to reach the impaled blade. But the weapon falls flat.

He grips the knife, cleans the stainless steel on his jeans,
pinches its tip between forefinger and thumb,
throws it level, like a line drive in a hardball game
when you don't have time to duck.
It sticks; she stretches.

This time she throws nearer in, committed
to finishing the game, conscious of the honed blade
and how easily it could slice to bone.
All she wants is to get the knife out of her hands.

Chicken. You throw like a girl!
He takes elaborate aim himself. Now the blade stands.

She inches one bare foot until, on legs extended
wobbly as clothes poles, she balances.

Her turn...His....
He aims to see how close he can come and still miss.

Not wanting to watch but without the courage to turn away,
she curls her toes, buries them in grass
as if those blades can shield her.

The muscles of her calves tighten,
their ache almost a distraction.
She prays that the knife will slip
and root so far away that she can't reach
no matter how hard she tries.

Blue Parakeet

You were the oldest,
fourteen, the father left behind;
you were the one who bore the brunt
of mother's misplaced rage.
When you left, I took your place.
We shared little except that.
Still I was surprised to see
how you twisted the neck of the cat
you'd had since it was a kitten
the day it tore the feathers and
split the skin of the sky blue parakeet
you'd let loose to fly around the house
and forgot to cage again,
the bird you'd finger-trained,
the one you whistled conversations to.

The Left Hind Foot

A Sunday afternoon sitting
on a neighbor's couch,
my father draped an arm
over my stiff shoulder, my back
erect, my eyes searching
for a place to look
so uncomfortable with the unfamiliar
closeness. Did he say
he loved me or just that
he'd kill any bastard
who laid his hands on me?
I was twelve.
And I believed him.
After all, how many times
had he cut the left hind foot,
the lucky one, off a rabbit
and given it to me
for being his good girl.

Soft-Mouthed

Pliers pulled the porcupine quills
from the black-and-tan's mouth.
His left arm locked the head
of his favorite hound tight to his ribs.
Coaxing with gentle words,
my father finished the job.

I suppose that sometime he talked
like that to me. Softly, gently,
just us two.
I'd like to think he did.

Celery

Muck land is what they called it,
the rich black loam needed for raising celery.
The girl didn't like squatting in the soil,
transplanting seedlings, patting the damp earth
to support thin stems. She was proud the summer
her uncle allowed her to work in the wash house,
standing full-aproned on the cool concrete,
hosing the virgin green clumps, slender leafed tops
rising out of lapped folds, washing the dirt
down a drain that flushed soil to the field.
She liked packaging the stalks in clear plastic,
packing the crates for storage in the coldroom—
that and the crate-making rooms, disquieting,
reserved for older boys and men.
She knew celeries' tender hearts
were worth more than the tougher, bigger stalks
that embraced them. What amazed her
was how white the hearts were
and how the seedlings could stand
so straight in the muck.

What My Mother Told Me

Rising moons on fingernails
bring wealth. Wide hips
brood babies well, but never
wear stripes across them.
A widow's peak may mean you're smart
but doesn't guarantee common sense.

Work never killed anyone
is a myth of the rich.
Wash floors on hands and knees,
rinse with vinegar, then wax.
To skin peaches and tomatoes
dip in boiling water, then in cold.
Wild berries make the best pies.

Wear hat and gloves when you go
downtown. Walk on the side
of the sidewalk away from the road.
When boys whistle, don't turn around.
Win, but don't cheat.
Watch out for men who do.

The Woodchuck's Lot

No one calls the woodchuck paranoid,
him with his maze of burrows,
holes like a bad case of acne
pocking the ground. Oh,
he stands bravely enough,
statuesque,
erect on the edge,
but he knows when to run
and moves deceptively fast
in spite of his fat,
skin rippling,
the wake of a ship
already gone past
or the pelt of a Fifth Avenue
lady's fur coat,
someone's idea of camouflage
or God's ill-fitting joke.
But we don't decry
his timidity,
may admire in fact
his ability to circum-
vent attack.

Pulling the Brass Handle

The top drawer of a tall oak dresser—
tarnished cuff links, linted change,
a keychain with plastic tubes where, tilted,
a milky film exposes full breasts of women,
jackknives whose blades tuck into slits or
skinning knives with steel sheathed in leather,
crow calls, varnished walnut cylinders
mouthed and blown, a blue-barreled revolver,
deliberate double action, no safety,
.38 bullets and casings scattered—
A man's place, a husband's, a father's.

Springing the Trap

You said the fox never felt the pain
when the No.2 bit into its leg,
tethered him by spike and chain
to frozen ground.

I wanted to believe
what you said was true.
It was more merciful to club him
than to shoot and mar his fur.

I even gathered walnuts for you
to stain the traps. You boiled
the hulls until the steel was tannic
and your face a smoky black.

You gave the traps such care,
waxing them, then hanging them
in the apple tree to air.
I watched you skin and stretch

the pelts, turn them inside-out.
I stood by at auction, silent,
as the lots were bought—
highest bids for prime pelts.

For years I was your accomplice
until I realized I traveled a trail
on which there was no doubling back.
How could I not have understood why
a fox will chew through its own foot
to escape the cutting edge.

First Night

Skinny fox, you came flying out of a cave,
   ears pointing, teeth bared, snapping at what
I held by one hand.

What was I doing with a heavy baseball glove,
   pocket worn, shaped to a hand that was not
mine, or was it....

In dreams maybe you can have those things
   you only dreamed of having—a glove, your own, not
borrowed, not your brother's.

And the man who stood off to one side, not
   disinterested, perhaps, this time. Just
too far away to help.

If not my father, who was he?

Releasing the Safety
Bad Dream

I am hiding in rooms.
I know you are searching.
You want others to look,
look out for my good.
Neighbors believe
there's no reason to fear
a man as reasonable as you,
but I do.

Other men come.
I won't let them stay.
I'm good
and don't let them near.
I sense that now
it's time to move on
to new rooms, bare
light bulbs and beds.

I walk cobbled streets.
You see me there;
I run back to the rooms,
up flights of stairs,
slam shut the door, hope
I'll be safe here.

Women wait in the rooms.
They listen. I think
they believe in my side.
Yet, just when I'm crouched

in a corner as deep as I can,
they nod to you, smiling
handsome and dark, relaxing
in the one comfortable chair.
The whole time you've been near.

For my own good, they say.
Even a psychiatrist,
tight dress shiny black,
sits on the edge of my single bed,
laughs at your jokes,
says take you back.
You say you'll take care
of me; you'll take me home
—or some other place,
just for a while.

You reach for the door,
and they never see
the .25 auto you cradle under your arm,
the snub-nose revolver you sleep near each night,
the 12 gauge pump shotgun propped in the corner,
or—on the day that I leave—
the .38 Wesson you wear holster open.

Clean Shot

They say when you kill
a deer, you should shoot it clean
to the neck or heart.
A quick death
without the panic of pain
that pumps adrenalin through
muscle walls, the spurt
of blood that diminishes
into a spotted trail,
before fear claims buff eyes
and flattens their hue.
A quick death—
else the taste turns wild.

Gutting the Deer

Begin at the asshole.
Cut around the balls.
Slit open the belly.
Pare, but don't puncture,
the sac. Spread fingers
to cradle the translucent
membrane, tough as a newborn's,
and lift out whole —
warm heart, liver, kidneys.
Save, if you wish.
Stand aside when intestines
shift, spill over
onto the frozen ground.
Last, free the full
saddlebag lungs.
More than seems possible
for the cavity
to contain.
Are we like this?
Once opened,
would we overflow?
This hole steams
with stories of men
crawling inside
to keep alive.
Or is it the soul
I see rising?

Red Mud

ink

a woman walks
                              on broken wings
          she has not learned
                              she cannot fly

                              a feathered quill
bends crushed   still
              its hollowed tip
                            does not run dry

oh   woman   woman
                        somehow you know
            inside you'll find
                          the sky

both black and blue
                    both wet and dry

Quail

I like to imagine the bobwhite quail
I released last spring are alive,
mated with offspring, coveyed together.
Not fallen prey to the red-tailed hawk
who lays claim to the towering white pine
and the fields within range
or to the gray fox whose footprints
muddy the creek bank or to the cars
that arc too fast around the curve
at the foot of my drive.
I'd like to believe something more
than chance ensures what will survive.

Deer

The deer meander
A lazy grazing
Across roads
Onto front lawns
Bathed
In headlight
Floodlight
Moonlight
Nearly spring night.
They almost invite me.
At least they don't spring away
But stare idly
Then saunter
Not far off
To another spot
Searching out grass
Waiting to green
Below earth's surface.
To be that earth!
Moist for the nuzzling
Bathed by steaming breath.

Moose Encounter

Had I been the moose disturbed from
my morning's mudding at the roadside bog,
perhaps I might have demonstrated

an equally indignant demeanor, imitated
his haughty stare, turned my rump,
and stiff-legged an ungracious exit.

What I'd interrupted was not some idle
wander, but an adolescent's abandoned romp,
hoof prints left like a housewife gone mad,

gouging rising dough. "Housewife", granted
a word near gone extinct, but one I suspect
embedded still in New Hampshire's granite hills.

For miles I had read the roadside signs
--Moose Crossing, 170 Collisions—
and heard the radio's dumb-moose jokes.

Not a likely beast to emulate.
Yet, how can I fail to admire an animal
who, given mud, makes pleasure of it.

Midsummer Night

The soft soaking rain has stopped.
A screen door sifts the metallic ring
of cricket and June bug to a finer hum.
This is a night when nothing
more seems needed
until the snorting snuffle
of some colossal beast intrudes.
Ten full minutes it romps and tromps,
shaking earth so nightcrawlers
dive for deeper cover.
A neighbor's mare
escaped from pasture to our greener
ground, her footfalls pound
and suck wet clods of clay.
Then she lifts tail and trots
down the road—owners trailing
close behind—leaving
the great pock-marked face
of what had been well tended lawn
warted, pug-nosed, cauliflower-earred.
What character it has!
How wonderful to be
such a beast, to bequeath
this cratered evidence.

I wrote a poem about meeting Allen Ginsberg,

that was after thinking about meeting Sharon Olds
on a train from DC to Philly. She was traveling
with Toi Derricote, and they got on at Baltimore
after doing a reading, but that didn't seem big enough
and I could tell she really didn't remember meeting me
earlier at the Dodge Poetry Festival at Waterloo,
but she mumbled I looked familiar, her head posed
down and to the side, shoulders hunched, like a sparrow
in a cage before she's used to capture.
I had a hunch she didn't really want to talk to me,
but the train was crowded and she needed a place to perch.
Then I thought about writing about chauffeuring Naomi Shihab
Nye; she was tired that night at Dodge and just glad
to have a ride back to the hotel although later she did record
for a project I was doing....she was really nice, and I guess
memories aren't made of that much anymore. Or about
having lunch with Paul Winter which led to using his Antarctica
music for an Ice art installation another time....pretty far removed
from the dinner with Stanley Kunitz when I was so nervous
about making conversation, I tipped over a candle and
set the table on fire. Of course, there were eight poets
at that round table and no danger with that many glasses
of water. Poets always have water handy though mostly what
they drink is wine. Poets seemed too predictable a subject,
and Sergeant Shriver came to mind. We shook hands once
long before my poet days....and D.H. Lawrence, whom
in fact was dead when I learned to drive a jeep, slept
in a bed at his Taos ranch, visited his grave and pretended
to be impressed, pretended I knew who he was. Lucille
Clifton didn't come to mind until later, the way we tend

to disregard those closest to us. Or David Ignatow
who walked around Yaddo's pond each night and asked
to read my poems. Lucille helped jury me into there, and there—
at Saratoga Springs—was Molly Peacock, too. Together we saw
the New York City Ballet perform, but I passed on going to the springs
for baths and massage, not wanting my legless leg exposed to view,
nor to give the reason why, but I remember what she said
about writing sonnets, that form gives her control over
what's most difficult for her to write about.
I am embarrassed to say I've never written a sonnet, though
I recall part of Shakespeare's *Let me not to the marriage of true
minds admit impediments....love is not love when.....*
I've not been good at remembering poems, even my own,
nor at loving, for that matter. But how could one fail
to love William Stafford; no, I can't call him Bill,
but I did eat spaghetti with him in a third floor walk-up
in Philly—more memorable than several
dinners later served on white linen tablecloths at Waterloo—
dumbstruck when he asked to hear the poems of us
seated on chairs and floor in a circle rather that read his own.
I managed a few lines of *Bear* before fumbling into silence,
but still with him I felt okay. In Philadelphia, too,
my first public reading there in the back side room
of a South Street bar where my friend Elizabeth and I had gone
to hear Etheridge Knight, and he cleared his friends and
had us sit in the front row....and then in the middle of his reading
asked each of us to read a couple of our poems,
and we did, and then he walked us back to the car because
it was late and not so safe at that end of South Street.
Years later I wished I had his company pulling into the parking lot
of Philly's North Star Bar. But by then, he was gone, hit by a car
on the street, wound up with cancer in a V.A. Hospital in Indiana.

I have his letters still. But how did I get back to poets
again? I did meet Paul Newman once. It was Molly Peacock
who introduced Elizabeth and me to him at *laura belle* on W. 43rd
where the Poetry Society held a benefit tribute to Stephen Sondheim.
We walked down the stairs to the round table where Paul sat
with Joanne and Steve and Mia, and we shook hands.
Later I made my way to stand next to him at the bar.
He is as short as they say, but how nice it was
those magic blue eyes that are bluer than legend
would have it were level with mine.
And though the paparazzi made most of Mia
Farrow's appearance—her first since leaving Woody—
and Sondheim autographed my program and I still have it,
today it's Newman's dressing I buy for my salad.

Numbers

Eighteen months
and I've not affixed
a number to my studio.
Neighborhood kids tagged
the brick building *86*
before I moved in.
I intend to remove it,
even tried once,
but it's still there.
My address is *97*.
I like the number.
The way it looks.
The way it sounds.
Finally, I gave my place a name:
Studio 97, after the address
97 Belmont, the corner
of Belmont and Erie.
But still no number
outside next to the door.
Nor my name, but somehow
that doesn't seem to matter
as much.
The old wooden *Fuel* sign
is whitewashed out.
A blank canvas of sorts,
appropriate enough
for an art studio. Notice
I say art, not artist's.
A steel beam arm protrudes
from the second story, the *Stable*

sign gone even longer
though not as long as
the horses that pulled loads of ice.
So there are opportunities—
places for my name
or at least the number.
People say they can't find me.
I say I'll put up a number soon,
look for the big blue tank
behind. At home
it's no better. No number
marks the house.
Fed-Ex and UPS
are always complaining.
Six years and counting.
The cabin I own in Michigan
has a number
I don't even remember.

The River Place

She came to the river place, not expecting to find love.
Just hoping for it.

As if those waters would leave it
washed up on her banks.

Nights she lay in bed, listening for his footsteps
above the rapids' rush.

She didn't hear them.
Only a rap at the door.

Opening, the solid stance of him
two paces behind a friend,

someone to keep them
a safe distance apart.

She couldn't have him, so she bought the river;
then, the woods;

and still it wasn't enough.
It made her smile though.

And she became quiet, almost content,
and not as old,

though life seemed shorter.

Flesh Tones

My belly's soft,
dough kneaded
to consistency,
no taut drum skin
empty echoing.
My womb's been filled,
twice cushioned life,
skin stretched
luminescent
as full moon.
Now inward folds
like pale pink petals
of wild morning glory,
not wilting on the vine,
convolvulaceous,
silken soft
this mellowing time.

Dear Laughter

You entered my life late
even though your sound surrounded
me in school rooms and hallways
and holidays with relatives.
I thought you were just a talent I didn't have,
wasn't naturally born to, a gene lacking.

Not surprising a conclusion if you knew
my mother, whom I don't remember laughing,
even with neighbors, although she enjoyed
their games of canasta, Scrabble, bridge—
each game more serious as decades passed.
My father drinking with his buddies laughed,
but not with my mother or us kids unless
he was telling a story in which he was the star.
Maybe it was his crooked teeth caged behind
a handsome face that inhibited my husband's laughter
although with others he, too, was a charming man.

Don't get me wrong, I smiled a lot.
But a smile is a surface thing, a mask
for people to admire, to mistake for friendliness,
to deflect attention from hazel eyes that turn color
with emotion, those bared windows to a soul.
Perhaps I was just insecure, so unsure
as not to trust the openness
of genuine laughter—spontaneous, silly,
released after forty years of closed lips.

Sometimes others may hear me laughing
with friends, but it is alone, curled on the couch,
watching a Drew Barrymore or Sophia Loren
romantic comedy, when I most surprise myself
and take delight in the open-throated
exclamatory sound of you
punctuating space.

Fox

There was no need to be sly
at the edge of the wood
within yards of a creek.
No reason to think
the hole rooted out
at the base of a tree
would not be safe.
That the discs padding
from the field and
out to the stream,
that the smooth slip
where the body entered
its underground pod,
that this packing of snow
would ever be noticed
among the veed
trails of deer.
Perhaps the shy partridge
who favor this place
made you secure
with dinner at your door.
A wise choice.
A place I would choose
for a home.
That's how I found you here.

Holey Tree

What I expected
when I discovered
that holey tree
was an extraordinary
woodpecker.
What I found
was common
—not even red-headed—
plugging away
at a ho-hum rate.
This tree must be
its life work.
Why else
one rotting tree,
limbless bottom to top,
peckered with holes
both BB-sized and
grand enough to fit a fist,
one that could topple
in a passing wind.
But hasn't.
Half-stripped of bark,
it's hard to tell,
but likely
it is a cedar.
That's what my uncle said.
Soft wood,
woodsy aroma,
sap-sucking grubs.
Perhaps this is

a family tree,
a holding passed
from father to son—
or are woodpeckers
matriarchal?
Do genes dictate
this urge to sculpt?
Yet, in a woodsful
why this tree?
My questions, of course.
I doubt the woodpecker
pondered motivation.
Hammering his holes
close up, intent
on the tree,
are his eyes open?
What does he see?
Below, fresh sawdust
sprinkled on snow.
And me.

Owl

He lifts off the mown grass
  brown wings in four foot span
   and glides low into the dense
    cover of woods. I know he nests
     back there. I heard his mate
      call to him last week when crows
       attacked and he decoyed them to
        a thicket aside. Even now I hear
         the rasping call of their young
          grown enough to fly but not to
           feed themselves. Perhaps that's
          what brings him to the field
         this morning when the sun is
        high, risking whatever horned
       owls risk besides derision of
      coal-coated throats. Perhaps the
     grass feels green and good
    beneath the weight of his
   great body. Perhaps there
  is something which calls
  the souls of predators
 from flight to solid
ground.

Five Feathers

I found five black crow feathers
today, an omen of better of things
than the lawn mower mired in the mud.
I meant well, racing the rain
over lush green that disguised
underground springs and rust clay.
I should have given up sooner
instead of spinning the Snapper's wheels
forward and reverse, scarring the lawn,
ruts reaching toward China, and my
pulling and shoving just rocking it deeper.
The truth is it didn't much bother me.
The hand mower started on the second pull.
I trimmed near an abandoned well,
found feathers, walked the field.
Not a bad evening. Not a bad life.

Turning Stones

For months I was content to sit alone and listen to a great
    horned owl *whooo* his mate.
Not so now.
I rush home to gather what light I can, pry rocks loose
    from rooted ground.
I've found, face down, stones nearly formed, fissured
    by a sculptor's chisel.
Perhaps the carver didn't want to be reminded of mistakes
Or simply liked to see an unhewn side in wild piles under
    pine.
For forty years he heaved out broken pieces; I've come to
    excavate.
It's late. I'm digging deeper.
The shovel tonks against granite's grain and pings metallic
    rock.
My body absorbs the tremors.
No stranger to slug and centipede, I keep my distance by
    wearing garden gloves,
One finger worn through where I dropped the wooden handle
And used my hands to dig and grip surfaces without clean
    edges, but
Like on the fuzzy edge of understanding one moment clearly,
I could not hold the wholeness, and it slipped away.
Where once I would have rocked the stone and set it back
    over burrows of golden ants,
I've become the homewrecker.
My mind churns to renovate a deserted slate patio into
    a garden of mistakes.
I leave the mud-crusted side facing sky for rain to clean
    earth's disguise
And return to turning stones.

Wild Turkeys

The wild turkeys flocking by the hundreds are an excuse she uses
to push herself up the road in air wind-chilled below zero.
Sun so brilliant against the snow she is blind to her own shadow.

Cresting the hill, she doesn't expect to see them strutting
across the road. Her squeaking bootsteps propel stragglers
to haul football bodies into short bursts of flight.

They land running a stiff-legged gait into the end zone
at the base of a tilled hill where they settle to glean.
This time she doesn't even make an effort to take count.

She zips her collar above her chin. Pulling in the reins
of her hood, she walks back into the peppered sting of snow.
At the cabin she checks her presence in a mirror.

Fingers trace the ridge of cheeks. She thinks of how
he would like their robust flush if he were there to see it,
how similar the surfaces of heat and cold.

Homecoming in February

Catalpa pods hang like brown tongues
from their mouths.
The snow they pawed to find them,
pocked with hoofprints.
                                    In my absence
they've worked their way close,
bedding within sight of the living
room, browsing my succulent
perennial garden.
                            I should fend them off,
but I don't want a repeat
of last winter's yearling,
its back to the stone's warmth,
starved under my kitchen window.
                                        Instead
I stand on the back slate patio,
heaving ears of corn, talking to the twenty
that scattered when I came with
the blue plastic pail.
                        Come....Be brave....I won't hurt you.
The cobs fall on the snow.
They don't sink. It's clear. It's cold.
The moon is full.
We are silhouette and shadow.

White

In a house of white walls
the woman writes
what happens
outside those walls.
She doesn't mention
the cupboard door
opening on its own.
The new furnace clanks
on and off.
She would like
the phone to ring.
But it doesn't.
Or to stop
thinking about
the absence.
She would like
to be satisfied
with herself.
Make a move
      to read something
          useful like
      Eighteen Songs
      of a Nomad Flute
          or
      Su-Tung Po
          or to look at
      Matisse's textured
      room with an empty bed
      and a window.
Now she knows why

the yellow notepad
seems necessary,
and the steady
hum of the furnace
blowing hot in her face.
It's the moon full
and white as the snow
in the field burning
through bubble-glassed
windows.
       Another moon....
           twenty moons and
                 somewhere she left
         the river rushes
         and a fox
         comes to drink
     and the moon is
         full and white and
    a man she loves
stands close enough
to see.

Rut

The deer are in rut.
They move through frosted stubble,
not furtive shadows, but silhouettes,
take stand, unflinching,
emboldened by their drives.

And mine? My urge is to burrow
deep, build fires, burn candles,
take you into my nest, curl
against the ridge of your spine,
body to bone.

To a Friend

We talk on the telephone
like teenagers, comparing notes,
detailing the littlest gestures
of our lovers, their smallest courtesies,
the grandeur of the passion
we've found again.
We drop our voices not to betray
the examples we've been careful to set
for adolescent daughters and sons.
Independent women who pay
the bills, change the oil,
listen to jazz live,
we hold our own
with humor, look better
than our children's best friends' mothers
--self-sufficient without sex.
But enter a man
whose touch unleashes desires
tamed twenty years past, and here we are
tracing new paths dot-to-dot
with unfamiliar freckles,
massaging muscles, tasting salt
--bittersweet, but knowing
sugar is no substitute.
How different from recipes
we've traded in the past,
lo-cal dips served at luncheons,
desserts to please our husbands.
For this potpourri
there are no measurements

to follow, no order given,
no sifting for a fine light taste.
This rises full-bodied.
We are gluttons without shame.

Temptation

We were seven and danced with seven
veils, shedding a cocoon of chiffon
scarves and sheer curtains.
We exposed our bared bellybuttons,
shifted hips like harem dancers
glimpsed at summer carnivals.
Imitating their sensuous movements
with little girl bodies, swaying,
tempting big brothers to touch.
We knew we were wicked.
Sneaked our performances
in Veronica's upstairs bedroom.
Charged two cents or one pop bottle
for the boys to see.
Sometimes we rehearsed for free.

Hybrids

These are not the red raspberries of my youth.
The fog-frosted, tender berries that stained a girl's
fingers. Not One-Armed Chris's tamed thorns
that scratched gently—enough to teach the lesson
that all sweet things have a price.

This is my first picking of the wild hybrids
that line the driveway and hold back the woods.
After rainfall and before the birds do their stripping,
leaving only flesh cones where ruby red should be,
I go out, as a novice would, bare armed, plastic container.

Even as a child, I knew enough
to wear denim and long sleeves and
to carry a berry bucket looped over my belt
to leave hands free, one for holding back the briars,
the other to pick the ripest berries hidden beneath.

At first I am alone.
I notice now what I never knew:
The way to pick is not to pick, but
to roll each nodular berry with the thumb
like a woman strokes her nipple, unconsciously or not.

The birds have found me out.
First a fluttering, then the call that summons.
It becomes the shrieking that smaller birds use
to drive a red-tailed hawk away. Except among the leaves
these birds remain anonymous; thus more threatening.

I think of Alfred Hitchcock's *Birds* and wonder
if their numbers grow, will they dare attack?
I pick one blue jay feather from the ground.
There is no guilt. Let them witness what they will.
The berries deeper in the tangled thicket can fill their caws.

I am all thumbs
excited at my new knowledge.
Then I am reminded of an older one—
When the briars prick, stay still and lift the stem,
Pulling away rakes the skin and the thorns hold harder.

What's in a Name

P, a promising beginning,
a prayer without the extra weight
of bowed head or bended knee.
Prominent, but not pendulous,
breasts, standing erect; posture
that would make my mother proud.
A woman any man might gladly
suckle, and two children have....
so long ago he might have been Adam—
the children, angels themselves
though occasionally fallen.
Ah, Time, so reckless a temptress.
*T*ravel and temptations too passed by
as if there would be another time.
*G*oodness knows, the brass ring
was there for the grabbing
if I'd dared reach...like the G spot
(is that the letter? so unfamiliar
though well within reach).
*O*r was it the other ring – the O
that formed like the mouth
forbidden to open, the silent
noose of omission, repeated each night in
*O*ur Fathers, over and over
until the line is drawn.
*D*rowning in Don't do's and duty
one becomes dumb.
Thank God for breath
at the syllable's end.
*R*ejoice at the R which gives

a slanted leg to stand on
and supports the breast,
Ribald, rich, real.
It moves me forward.
I can almost believe in the equality
of an isosceles triangle and the identity
of the individual, the I that strikes,
not the middle *C*, no half-way note,
but higher, vaulting the horizontal bar
off the page... two legs connected
wHole.
*H*allelujah!

Directions for Maps Without Boundaries

Walk past a mill where men guide
logs through machines.

Scavenge rusted bands
of metal strapping, kinked and curved.

Lightly scour the surface rust—
let the patina remain

not unlike mottled, fine-lined skin.
Rub each strip by hand.

Lay them out on a table, vertical
and horizontal, uncentered,

long limbs reaching unevenly, curving
downward or outward; leave holes between to fill in,

if imagination desires, with Mondrian erector-set colors.
Weave and rivet here and there,

just enough to give body, always leaving a corner undone—
the possibility of a thread pulled unraveling warp and woof.

Include the warped.
Let them form their own topography

in this dance of line and curve.
Last, add the oddity,

a twisted band or one whose thickness sets it apart.
Play and take pride.

See them for what they were:
rusted,

a topography of holes, the plywood factory
at the end of the block, a burrowing child

making tunnels through banded sheaves of strips,
or potholders latch-hooked on a metal loom,

two for a quarter, sold house to house
even after the lights came on.

Locus

I.

A chunk of sky moves

Not the blinding God of mountain and burning bush

Here the torch is a sienna tree whose rootedness you cannot see

And in the distance
In the distance
Thin
Blue

II.

That is not the angled world I see.
It is all above me.
I am the creature out of the painting.
Below at the base of the burnished tree,
Below where snow has riven into rivulets,
I cup palms and drink,
And my feet follow the spoor of deer and elk.
And the bear has scratched its mark,
Left its smell, grubbing a feast,
Shredding cedar's sweet decay,
Wading the river's rush,
Working its way
Down the mountain,
Below
Where green holds ground.

The Way Home

At last I plant my foot in grass again.
Half expecting the blades to cut,
I dig in and curl my toes as if
they were roots of some exotic walking tree.

How long it's been since I've walked barefoot
across the lawn, sinking flat-footed into
the smooth green coolness of shaded patches,
arching so only the ball of my foot is stung

by the stubble of sun worn spots.
You might think that with one real foot
I would have savored such feeling
as often as I could. Instead for years

I have taken cover, worn shoes to protect the good sole,
to keep balance with the stiff-ankled wooden foot,
its pitch permanently set for low-heeled shoes,
its heel inset with rubber, giving bounce to my step,

cushioning the hard, deliberate heel-to-toe roll,
a roll that turns rocky if both feet are not shoed.
But today (I'm not sure why) it doesn't seem to matter—
not even if my gait is uneven or if I stumble and fall.

My arch shapes itself to the contour of the lawn,
riding the pitch and roll of its waves.
Each toe greets grass and dandelion, old friendships
renewed as skin remembers their touch.

How much more connected I am
without that half inch of leather between.
Is this how a mare feels spring-wild in a meadow,
unshod hooves massaging the earth!

In Praise of the Dolphin

To talk of butchering a dolphin on the beach
seems to trivialize it, but to understand
the skull and bones sunning on my slate patio,
you need to have seen it first
from a distance, the carcass washed ashore,
its great head curled like the crest of a wave,
looking out to sea, one flipper beckoning,
the other leaning into the sand, a crooked seating,
albeit one with dignity.
                              You would know then,
my first impulse was not to turn away,
but to admire the graceful vertebrae
and wonder where the great lower jaw,
the smile giver, had gotten to,
and why so few ribs remained.
                              I might have walked away
satisfied with those few links. Instead,
there was a furtive burying, saving the body
for a return with friends,
and the dismembering we visited upon it
to harvest the skull and scapula,
the backbones and ribs.
                              The thick, black hide
resisted the blade of a butcher knife.
White worms and dark maggots erupted.
Avoiding those areas of infestation and decay,
three of us took turns sawing, thankful
for the strong wind that carried the stench away.
We purified the remains
in buckets bubbling with bleach.

Then soaked ourselves in salt water—
two artists and I
                    laughing, released,
glad to be rolled by the waves, carried
in their curl, reckless women, pulled by an undertow.
My shed prosthesis, left safe behind, now far down shore.
Picture-taking, me legless
for the first time in a photo, a lop-sided
mermaid smiling between friends.
The photographer, a composer, keeping a measured distance.
                    Finally, we all kneeled,
scooping sand with purple and pearl clam shells
to keep the entrails from marauding gulls and fiddler crabs.
A painter, who had washed his own father's bones
in a ritual of respect as a boy in China,
staked a driftwood cross.
We circled the mound with shells and our own bodies.
Fists funneled sand, thumbs pointing up.

Woodchuck

He lay there, light belly
up, paws cupped to the sky,
not stiff on his side,
legs extended
as roadkills often do.
It was near an exit ramp,
and I thought of how
another poet might stop his car
and lovingly observe him,
weep over his soft fur,
cry for the curl of his toes
never again to burrow
earth's bowels, save him
to be immortalized in some poem.
And I wished I could write
those extravagant words,
make an extravagant gesture,
live an extravagant life,
risk crossing roads,
be fully animal,
be fully alive.
Even in death
cupping hands
both in supplication
and as if catching
rain or manna.

Fragments of Bone

Worm paths etch skinned pine.
We have a common language.
Snow traces patterns of retreat.
Thick lies the dew.

Too much is here.
Do not go far from my heart!
Hear the wind before it's seen.
Pure is the white pony.

Pennies worn thin, left to ground.
Now the morning star shines bright.
One blue flag marks a new beginning
                near the water hole.
The willow's at the last gate.

Elegant curved leg, green velvet,
Pretending to be overcome by shyness.
Look beyond the gnarled root dancing
                with golden stone.
She is gathering lotus seed in the rivers of Yahweh.

Coins secreted in pockets. I am that child.
So hard to speak of it.
Fresh ruts—crisscrossing treads.
The red has parted from the green.

Concrete bear or badger, incomplete
As he follows the horse, wondering, wandering.
Snow creeps back to the shadow of stone wall.
Winter is gone, and spring returns.

Lichen scribbled green on stone
To write me a poem calling me to return.
Silver winged creatures, feelers forward.
Over the melancholy river thousands
                    of peaks are folded

Sawdust scattered, sculpture abandoned.
I am more.
Red mud, fresh tracks,
An empty can on a rock,

White shard of bone
Whose days are numbered. Hallelujah!
Crows Caw Caw Caw Cawl
What kind of a person are you?
                    I hear them say to me.

Ice Defined

Ice. Three letters. One little word.
I stand, a girl from Northern Michigan,
on the cement porch of a green shingled house,
watching the icicles drip diamond water, waiting
for my dad to break one off for me. Warned
not to lick it, it becomes my Ice Princess wand
while another becomes my big brother's sword.
At least that is what I want to remember.

Ice is skating at Diggins Park,
mitted hands lacing second-hand skates bought
at White's Hardware store. I arch my back, lean into being
a swan. Crossing arms across my breastless chest,
I hold myself into a Sonya Henje spin, wishing I had
a skating skirt and wool tights instead of flannel-lined
jeans, but thankful for a sunny day's thaw and
below-zero night that polishes ice.

Ice is fishing on Lakes Cadillac
and Mitchell, a hole sawed out, a window
into the world of water deep and dark.
My snow-panted bottom balancing on an overturned bucket.
Me, wiggling double-socked toes, trying not to stamp feet,
watching a tip-up pole, sipping hot chocolate from a thermos,
envious of the kids following their dads out of the wind
into ice shanties with heaters and blanketed benches.

I learned to listen to ice—
its groan, squeak, crack; the deep echo
before it explodes. And to avoid black ice

---

where springs and creeks that feed the lakes
push against the boundaries ice imposes,
where despite a smooth surface
the ice is unstable and can't be trusted.
Kids fall through and so do cars. I am cautious.

There is a season of ice.
Married with a newborn son, I join neighbors
in Vanscoy, Saskatchewan, celebrating New Years,
the date that marks when days stay below zero and,
as if hockey weren't enough, teams of husbands and wives,
old friends and new, grandparents and grandchildren
dust off their brooms and sweep down the village
curling rink, its ice frozen clear and solid for the season.

Ice is blue and I am solitary
on a glacier. A helicopter waits nearby,
but it cannot take away this immensity of being
above the cloud line high on an Alaskan mountain,
thin air, sun blinding, white snow and strata wisps,
blue sky and ice, a trickle of water cutting a crevasse,
space enough to almost dissolve
into God.

Another River Place

The women of my family didn't understand
when I showed them the robe wrapped around me
made from animal skin, the one I had climbed
a mountain for and the old woman allowed me to keep.
My mother, her sister my aunt Maryanne, sister-in-law
Karen, others I do not recognize but know
they've passed and somehow we're all related
are not impressed when I say, *I am fine here. I can stay.*
See the old woman has a chair by the creek. Yes,
there was a creek, its water flowing, and the old woman
standing there near a blue fiberglass chair, smooth curves
shaped to hold a body like the purple leather chair
Mother had for years on the green concrete front porch,
the chair her feral cats curled on like guards at an Egyptian tomb,
and even though it was cracked and stained,
I brought home and put on my side porch by the kitchen door.
That purple chair, the one thing I wanted after she died.
The chair is not close to the creek, someone said. And another,
There is a sign on the seat. She cannot even sit there.
They turned and walked away down the gravel road.
It was true: A white sheet of paper I had read from a distance,
Danger—Toxic.... and chose to ignore.
I said to them, though they may not have heard
or just weren't listening. *It's okay.*
It doesn't matter. I'll be fine.
And when the old woman looked at me
was her face filled with pity or just wrinkled by time?
I knew she would not stay, but I was glad
I had the cloak to wrap around me.

The Design

I'm not sure who told me
about leaving a place

for spirits to escape.
It doesn't matter:

What matters is this basket,
made it Lesotho, land of jarcarandas,

encircled by, but apart from, South Africa.
Its coiled reeds shade from sand to clay

to loam, follow a pattern that zigs and
zags over dragon-spined mountains,

desert and veldt, urn shaped
with a lid that tightly fits,

perfectly woven, but for
one deliberate flaw

where the sand runs dry
and pattern breaks design.

Here the maker admits his frailty.

This is the place that draws the eye,
that lets the spirit out.

Patricia Goodrich is a poet and visual artist. She has been featured reader at writers' conferences, including the Druskininkai International Festival, Lithuania, and the Geraldine R. Dodge Poetry Festival, USA. Her work has been translated into Chinese, Lithuanian and Romanian. She is Pennsylvania's 2005 Bucks County Poet Laureate. She is a recipient of fellowships through the Andy Warhol Foundation, Atlantic Center for the Arts, Europos Parkas (Lithuania), Inter-Art Foundation (Romania) Leeway Foundation, Makole Sculpture Symposium (Slovenia), Puffin Foundation, Santa Fe Art Institute, Vermont Studio Center, and Yaddo. Goodrich also received Pennsylvania Fellowships in Poetry/Creative Nonfiction and was nominated for Pushcart Prizes in poetry and fiction.

Printed in the United States
140516LV00002B/89/P